This book belongs to

....

LET'S TALK ABOUT
DINOSAURS

Illustrated by Britta Teckentrup
Text by Harriet Blackford

Boxer Books®

Contents

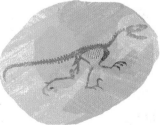

What are dinosaurs?

Some dinosaurs were the biggest animals ever to walk the earth.

Dinosaurs lived millions of years ago, long before there were people.

Earth looked very different then. Just one big piece of land surrounded by sea.

The name "dinosaur" means "terrible lizard".

Have you ever seen dinosaur bones in a museum?

Big and little dinosaurs

Brachiosaurus was as tall as three giraffes on top of one another.

How many elephants would it take to play seesaw with this Brachiosaurus?

Eoraptor was about the same size as a child like you.

Stegosaurus was as big as a truck, but its brain was the size of a ping-pong ball.

9

On the land

Gigantic dinosaurs roamed
the land looking for food.

Big plant eaters swallowed stones
to help grind down the tonnes
of plants they ate.

A Diplodocus' tail was as long as its neck.

Can you imagine the size of their poo?

Hunting dinosaurs

Tyrannosaurus rex, or T.rex, was a giant biting machine.

T.rex hunted other dinosaurs for dinner.

Fierce raptors hunted
in packs.

A raptor's claw was
bigger than your hand!

Head-butting dinosaurs

These dinosaurs are called Pachycephalosaurs. Their name means "thick-headed reptiles".

Some had bumps
or spikes to chase
away meat-eating
dinosaurs.

Dinosaurs with horns

Ceratopsians had huge heads, bony neck frills and horns.

Triceratops was as big as an elephant.

It had three horns on the front of its head.

Styracosaurus had
horns all around
its neck frill.

Dinosaurs with armour

Plant-eating dinosaurs had tough bodies so meat eaters would have a hard time eating them.

Ankylosaurus was covered with hard, flat spines and its tail was shaped like a club.

Stegosaurus had bony back plates and a spiky tail.

Watch out, T.rex. One bang from that tail and you could get hurt!

Fancy crests

Hadrosaurs had hollow head crests that could probably make a loud booming sound.

We think Hadrosaurs lived together in herds and would make a loud boom to warn everyone if a meat-eating dinosaur was close by.

Hadrosaur parents made nests for their babies.

Feathered dinosaurs

Some dinosaurs had feathers and ran on their back legs like birds.

Archaeopteryx was a bird that lived in dinosaur times. It had feathers but its teeth and tail were like a dinosaur's.

Velociraptor was a fearsome bird-like dinosaur. It had a long curved toe claw.

Think about Velociraptor when you see birds run across the grass.

Under the sea

When dinosaurs ruled the land, huge reptiles lived in the sea.

Plesiosaurs had very long necks and caught fish to eat.

Ichthyosaurs looked
a lot like dolphins.

Liopleurodon's
jaws were longer
than a canoe.

Doesn't giant
Deinosuchus look a lot
like a crocodile?

In the air

In the time of the dinosaurs the skies were filled with flying reptiles called Pterosaurs.

Some were as big as a small aeroplane. Some were as small as a sparrow.

26

Pterosaur wings were made of thin skin. But they had no feathers.

They had beaks with teeth to catch many different kinds of food.

What sort of sounds do you think they made?

27

Nesting on cliffs

Pterosaurs probably nested on cliffs like seabirds do today.

They could launch themselves into the air from the edge of a cliff and soar out over the sea.

Their eggs and babies would be safe while they hunted for food.

Would you like to be able to soar like a Pterosaur?

Baby dinosaurs

Some dinosaur eggs were as big as footballs. Some were as small as a chicken's egg.

Some mother dinosaurs covered their eggs with soft soil and left them to hatch on their own.

Triceratops may have formed a circle round their babies for protection.

Some dinosaurs, like Maiasaura, may have cared for their babies in nests.

More giants

Here are some really big dinosaurs with really big names.

Mamenchiasaurus was a huge plant eater.

Carcharodontosaurus was a giant meat eater.

Iguanodon was a giant plant-eating dinosaur with a huge spike on its thumb.

Where did all the dinosaurs go?

The dinosaurs disappeared about 65 million years ago.

Some scientists think a gigantic meteorite crashed into Earth.

Clouds of dust would have blocked out the sun.

With no sun the plants would die and the big plant eaters would have nothing to eat.

When the plant eaters died, the meat eaters would have nothing to eat either. All the dinosaurs would have died out.

How do we know about dinosaurs?

Scientists learn about dinosaurs when they discover fossils. Fossils are bones and other parts that have turned to stone over thousands of years.

When scientists find a fossil, they try to put the bones together to see what the animal looked like.

Dinosaur eggs, footprints and even poo can turn to stone over many thousands of years.

First published in Great Britain in 2009
by Boxer Books Limited.
www.boxerbooks.com

Boxer® is a registered trademark of Boxer Books Limited

This abridged edition published in 2015

Text copyright © 2009 and 2015 Boxer Books Limited
Original text written by Harriet Blackford
Illustrations copyright © 2009 Britta Teckentrup

The illustrations were prepared using hand-printed paper and digital collage.
The text is set in Avenir.

ISBN 978-1-910126-41-7

1 3 5 7 9 10 8 6 4 2

Printed in China

All of our papers are sourced from managed forests and renewable resources.

MORE BOOKS IN THIS FUN, YOUNG AND INFORMATIVE SERIES.

LET'S TALK ABOUT
ANIMALS
Britta TECKENTRUP

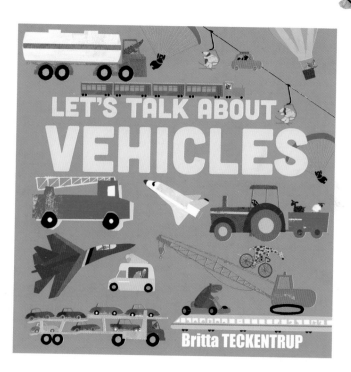

LET'S TALK ABOUT
VEHICLES
Britta TECKENTRUP